**ANIMAL FAMILIES**

 W9-ARX-662

PENGUINS
LIFE IN THE COLONY

Willow Clark

PowerKiDS press

New York

Published in 2011 by The Rosen Publishing Group, Inc.
29 East 21st Street, New York, NY 10010

Copyright © 2011 by The Rosen Publishing Group, Inc.

All rights reserved. No part of this book may be reproduced in any form without permission in writing from the publisher, except by a reviewer.

First Edition

Editor: Jennifer Way
Book Design: Julio Gil

Photo Credits: Cover, back cover, pp. 9 (top left), 11 (top), 15, 20–21, 23, 24 (bottom right) Shutterstock.com; pp. 5, 6–7, 24 (top right) Tom Brakefield/Stockbyte/Thinkstock; pp. 8, 9 (top right, bottom right), 10–11 (main), 17, 19 iStockphoto/Thinkstock; p. 9 (bottom left) Jupiterimages/Photos.com/Thinkstock; pp.12–13, 24 (bottom left) David Tipling/Getty Images; p. 24 (top left) Doug Allan/Getty Images.

Library of Congress Cataloging-in-Publication Data

Clark, Willow.
   Penguins : life in the colony / by Willow Clark. — 1st ed.
      p. cm. — (Animal families)
   Includes index.
   ISBN 978-1-4488-2510-3 (library binding) — ISBN 978-1-4488-2606-3 (pbk.) — ISBN 978-1-4488-2607-0 (6-pack)
   1. Penguins—Juvenile literature. 2. Penguins—Life cycles—Juvenile literature. 3. Familial behavior in animals—Juvenile literature. I. Title.
   QL696.S47C53 2011
   598.47—dc22
                                    2010019392

Manufactured in the United States of America

CPSIA Compliance Information: Batch #316260PK: For Further Information contact Rosen Publishing, New York, New York at 1-800-237-9932

CONTENTS

Penguins come together in a group called a **colony**.

A penguin colony meets up in the same place year after year.

There are 17 kinds of penguins. The emperor penguin is the largest penguin.

Gentoo Penguin

Adélie Penguin

Emperor Penguin

Rockhopper Penguin

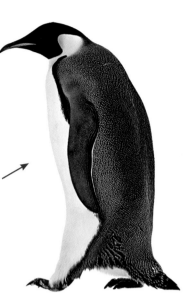

Chinstrap Penguin

9

The emperor penguin is the only animal that lives on Antarctica year-round.

Antarctica

11

Emperor penguins **huddle** together. They take turns getting warm in the middle.

Penguins find **mates** within their colony. The female penguin lays an egg.

Penguin parents take turns keeping the egg warm in their **brood pouches**.

16

A chick comes out of the egg. Its parents hold the chick in their brood pouches.

The chicks huddle together while their parents look for food.

The chicks leave the colony to find their own food when they are older.

Words to Know

brood pouch

colony

huddle

mates

Index

Web Sites

Due to the changing nature of Internet links, PowerKids Press has developed an online list of Web sites related to the subject of this book. This site is updated regularly. Please use this link to access the list:

www.powerkidslinks.com/afam/penguin/

24